THE LIFE CYCLE OF A

FERN

By L. L. Owens

Published by The Child's World®
1980 Lookout Drive
Mankato, MN 56003-1705
800-599-READ
www.childsworld.com

The Child's World®: Mary Berendes, Publishing Director
The Design Lab: Kathleen Petelinsek, design
Red Line Editorial: Editorial direction

Photographs ©: Bigstock, cover (top left, bottom right), 1 (top left, bottom right), 31 (middle); Alan Lagadu/iStockphoto, cover (top right, bottom left), 1 (top right, bottom left), 3; Shutterstock Images, 5, 9; Todd Boland/Shutterstock Images, 6; Carsten Reisinger/Shutterstock Images, 10; ScienceFoto/Photolibrary, 13, 30 (top); Dr. Richard Kessel & Dr. Gene Shih/Getty Images, 14, 18, 30 (bottom), 31 (bottom); Andre Mueller/Shutterstock Images, 17; Tischenko Irina/Shutterstock Images, 21; Olga Lipatova/Shutterstock Images, 22; Hervé Lenain & Marie-Pierre Samel/Photolibrary, 25; iStockphoto, 26, 29, 31 (top)

ISBN: 978-1-60973-149-6
LCCN: 2011927737

Printed in the United States of America
Mankato, MN
July 2011
PA02089

T A B L E   O F

CONTENTS

LIFE CYCLES

Every living thing has a life cycle. A life cycle is the steps a living thing goes through as it grows and changes. Humans have a life cycle. Animals have a life cycle. Plants have a life cycle, too.

A cycle is something that happens over and over again. A life cycle begins with the start of a new life. It continues as a plant or creature grows. And it keeps going as one living thing creates another, or **reproduces**— and the cycle starts over again.

A fern's life cycle has several steps: it starts as a spore, then grows and changes into a mature fern.

Like all living things, ferns have a life cycle.

Cinnamon ferns can often be found in moist, shady forests.

FERNS

Ferns are ancient plants that grew in the forests where dinosaurs walked. These plants have leaves, but no flowers or seeds. Fern leaves are called fronds.

There are more than 10,000 kinds of ferns. They live on every continent except Antarctica. Some are as small as a violet, but others grow as tall as trees. Many kinds grow in wet places like rain forests and wetlands.

Cinnamon ferns can be found in some backyards or wooded areas. And many people keep Boston ferns as houseplants.

SPORES

The life cycle of new ferns begins in spring when mature ferns make spores. A spore is living plant matter that is inside a tough case. A single spore may be as small as a speck of dust. Millions grow in clusters on the undersides of fern fronds. The clusters of mature spores look like small dots. They may grow in rows, stripes, or patches, depending on the kind of fern.

Fern spores grow on the undersides of fronds.

Dark fern spores are ready to be released by a fern.

Fern spores help ferns reproduce. Spores ripen in a few days or weeks and are then ready to leave their parent plant. On a dry day, they blow away on the wind. The breeze helps spread the spores to new places. Ferns can release millions or even billions of spores during their lives.

Spores may not land in the perfect spot right away. But they can survive a long time after they leave their parent plant. Spores can last months or even years. And they are too small to interest any animals that might eat seeds. Their ability to survive and travel so easily is one reason why ferns are found all over the world.

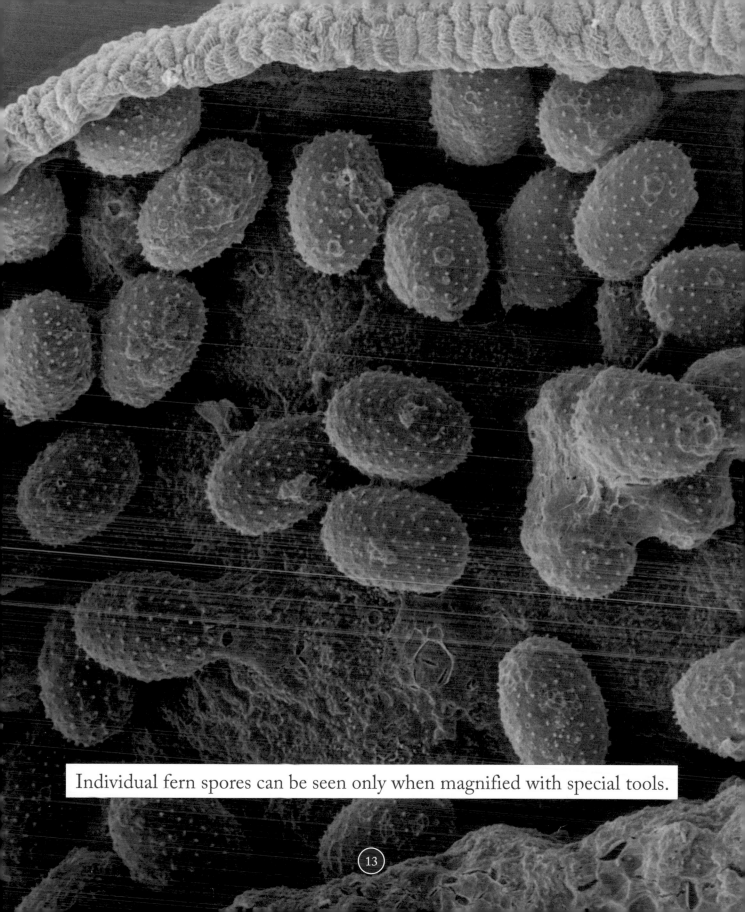

Individual fern spores can be seen only when magnified with special tools.

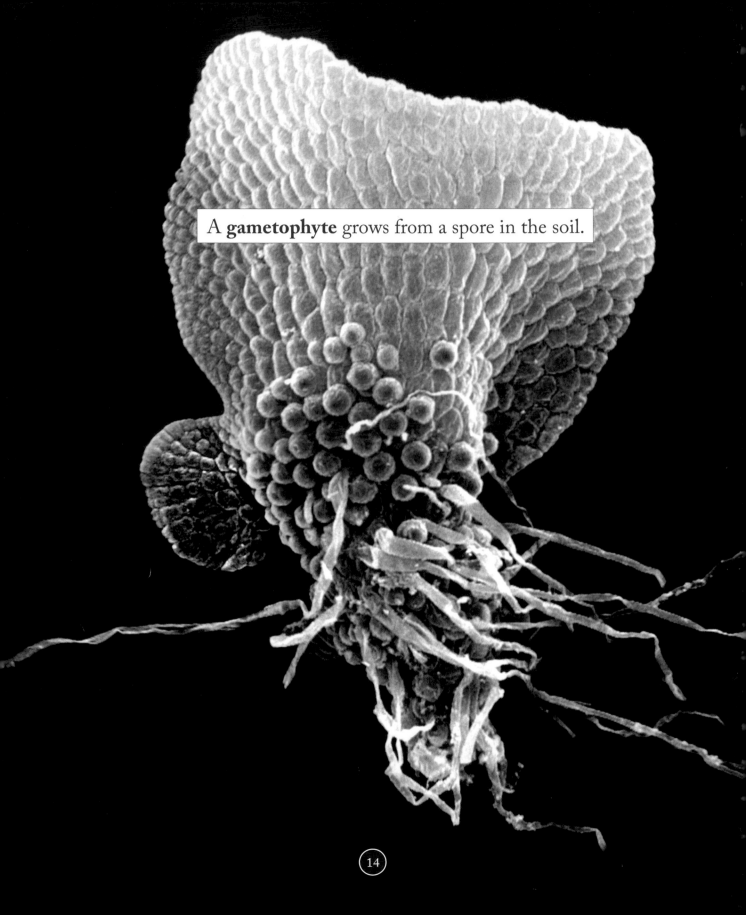

A **gametophyte** grows from a spore in the soil.

GROWING INTO A FERN

A moist, shady spot on the ground is best for spores. They settle onto the soil's surface. With some sun and water, they start to grow. They quickly grow into small, heart-shaped gametophytes.

Gametophytes look like thin green film, about the size of a pencil eraser. On the soil's surface, they look like tiny plants. Gametophyte roots grow down into the soil to search for moisture.

PLANTS MAKE FOOD

Gametophytes survive through a process called **photosynthesis**. Through this process, plants use light energy to create their food. Gametophytes trap the sunlight they need to grow food. The food made by green plants also makes them nutritious for other creatures. Some caterpillars and other animals like to eat gametophytes.

Caterpillars like to eat green plants for the food inside them.

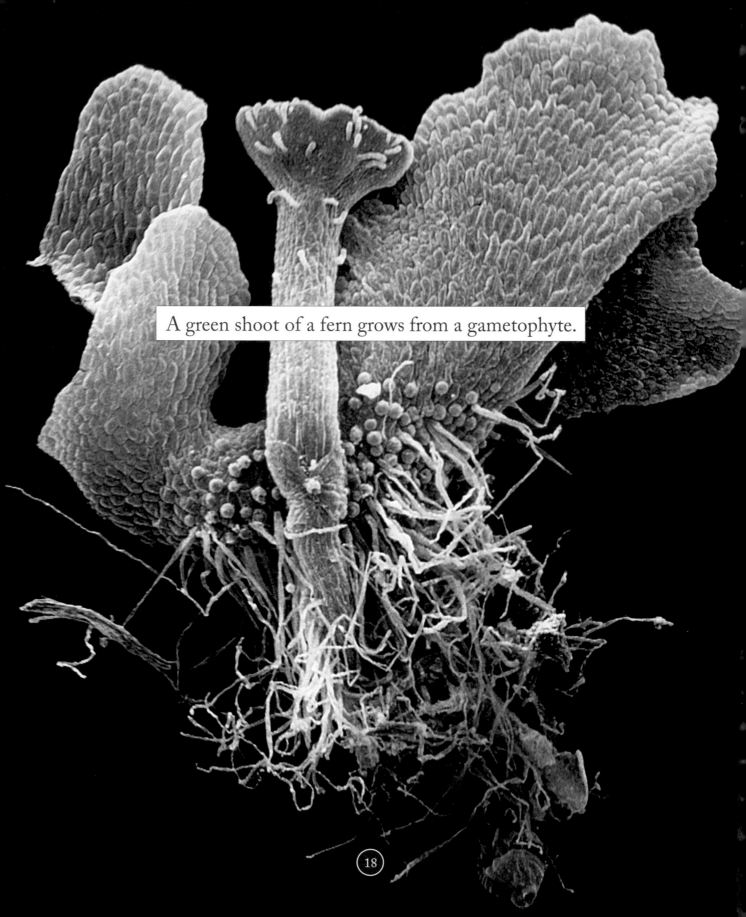

A green shoot of a fern grows from a gametophyte.

MAKING FERNS

For new ferns to grow, the gametophytes must reproduce. They do not have blooms that can make seeds like flowering plants. Instead, each tiny gametophyte develops male and female **reproductive** parts. The reproductive parts are located on the undersides of the plant. Each male part produces many sperm, and each female part produces an egg.

The next step is for the sperm to meet the eggs. Sperm are able to swim to the eggs only when a thin film of water is left under the plants by rain or dew. With the right amount of water, sperm glide across the plants. They then **fertilize** the eggs. Sperm and eggs may come from the same gametophyte or from different gametophytes.

Dewdrops and rain help gametophytes reproduce.

A **fiddlehead** is a young fern frond.

Next, a tiny young fern sprouts from the gametophyte. The new growth is called a **sporophyte** in the fern life cycle. Very small roots grow down in the soil. Then a green shoot appears above the ground.

Young fern fronds emerge from the green shoot in the soil. They are coiled like the ends of violins. These young ferns are called fiddleheads. The green fronds use photosynthesis to make food for the whole plant.

If the fern takes in too much sunlight during this time, its young fronds will dry out and shrivel up. The plant may die. Lack of rain can kill the fern, too. But with a good balance of moisture and light, new fern fronds stay healthy.

Below or above the ground, **rhizomes** grow from fern plants. They soak in water and other nutrients. Fern fronds also grow from rhizomes in spring.

A squirrel's foot fern has fuzzy rhizomes.

The big royal fern is found in North America.

MATURE FERNS

As the plant grows and thrives, its coiled leaves open up. Eventually they become the strong leaves of a mature fern. Fern leaves taste bad to many animals. But some insects, rabbits, and other creatures turn fern fronds into meals.

In cold weather, many kinds of ferns lose their fronds just like oak trees drop their leaves. But Christmas ferns hold onto their fronds even in the snow.

Ferns can live a long life. Most fern types live ten years. The royal fern is the largest in North America. It can live up to 100 years!

The next part of a fern's life cycle goes back to its beginning. In spring, new fiddleheads poke out of the soil and uncurl. When the fronds of the mature fern are full grown, spore clusters form on their undersides. When the spores ripen, they blow away on the wind.

Spores that land in good spots have a chance to help new ferns grow. The life cycle of the fern continues.

In spring, new fern fronds grow.

LIFE CYCLE DIAGRAM

Spore

Gametophyte

30

Mature Fern

Fiddlehead

Sporophyte

Web Sites

Visit our Web site for links about the life cycle of a fern:
childsworld.com/links

Note to Parents, Teachers, and Librarians: We routinely verify our Web links to make sure they are safe and active sites. So encourage your readers to check them out!

Books

Levine, Shar, and Leslie Johnstone. *Plants: Flowering Plants, Ferns, Mosses, and Other Plants*. New York: Crabtree Publishing, 2010.

Loves, June. *Ferns*. Philadelphia: Chelsea Clubhouse, 2005.

Pascoe, Elain. *Plants Without Seeds*. New York: PowerKids Press, 2003.

Glossary

fertilize (FUR-tuh-lyz): To fertilize is when a male reproductive cell joins a female reproductive cell to create a new life. Water helps the male part of a fern fertilize the female part.

fiddlehead (FID-uhl-hed): A fiddlehead is the young, curled frond of a fern. A fiddlehead uncurls as it grows.

gametophyte (ga-MEE-tah-fite): In the fern life cycle, a gametophyte is a small, green, heart-shaped plant that produces male and female reproductive cells. A fern spore grows into a gametophyte.

photosynthesis (foh-toh-SIN-thuh-siss): Photosynthesis is a process within green plants that changes light energy into food energy. Photosynthesis makes the food a fern uses to grow.

reproduces (ree-pruh-DOOS-ez): If an animal or plant reproduces, it produces offspring. A fern reproduces through spores and gametophytes.

reproductive (ree-pruh-DUCK-tiv): A reproductive cell or body part is used in making new creatures. A gametophyte has reproductive parts.

rhizomes (RY-zomes): Rhizomes are parts of plants that grow into or above the ground and which shoots of plants grow from. Fern fronds can grow from rhizomes.

sporophyte (SPORE-ah-fite): A sporophyte is the spore-producing part of the fern life cycle. A sporophyte grows from a gametophyte.

Index